CW01020374

Tunisian Crochet Handbook

A Step-By-Step Guide for Beginners in Stitching Tunisian Crochet Patterns With Tools and Techniques Included

By

Zera Meyer

Disclaimer

This publication is designed to provide competent and reliable information regarding the subject matter covered. However, the views expressed in this publication are those of the author alone, and should not be taken as expert instruction or professional advice. The reader is responsible for his or her own actions.

The author hereby disclaims any responsibility or liability whatsoever that is incurred from the use or application of the contents of this publication by the purchaser or reader. The purchaser or reader is hereby responsible for his or her own actions.

Table of Contents

Introduction

Interestingly, you have decided to take a step further in crocheting by getting a hold of this Tunisian crochet handbook to learn a creative crafting technique that has gained prominence worldwide. The most effective way to describe this crocheting technique is that it is the "holy matrimony" between knitting and crochet, but it is even easier than both.

In this handbook, emphasis would be laid on learning the Tunisian crochet craft in all its beauty and splendor. Perhaps you have been wondering if it's complex to learn? No, it is not. However, it will serve you better if you have prior knowledge of traditional crocheting since they both share some similarities in their terms and processes. This book will provide you with insight into what Tunisian crochet is. You will be educated on the craft's historical evolution and uncover the differences between Tunisian and conventional crochet.

In chapter 2, we will discuss several tips and tricks that will come in very handy in your journey. Your knowledge and acquaintance with them will help prevent you from making mistakes many beginners make. We shall be setting the ball rolling in chapter 3, where you will be learning the tools and materials required of this craft.

Just to make sure you're not left in the dark, you will get yourself acquainted with the charts, symbols, and abbreviations involved in Tunisian crochet. Chapter 4 will be more practical than every other chapter. It is the most elaborate because you will be taking up several Tunisian crochet projects. You will learn how to make ear warmers, washcloths, coffee sleeves, beanies, cowls, and other pieces.

In chapter 5, you will learn how to fix common Tunisian crochet mistakes encountered in your Tunisian crochet journey.

So, let's jump right into it.

Chapter 1

The Fundamentals of Tunisian Crochet

What is Tunisian Crochet?

Needlework is a vital component of the fashion industry. It's a broad spectrum covering crafts like sewing, embroidery, knitting, and crocheting. Nevertheless, crocheting is an awesome craft amongst them. Tunisian crochet, also called Afgan crochet, is widely considered a combination of knitting and crocheting. So, essentially, it provides the best of both needlework techniques. Tunisian crochet is done with a single hook, yet all the stitches are made with that hook, just like knitting. Several stitches and pattern combinations can be produced using Tunisian crochet.

Thick waffle-like fabric is usually produced from Tunisian crochet, making it suitable for afghans and projects that are ideal for cold weather. Tunisian crochet is also good for sturdy and durable projects such as blankets, washcloths, and dish towels.

Tunisian Crochet: A Short History

The history of Tunisian crochet has remained uncertain over the years. Surprisingly, no one knows where it came from and despite the name, there's no certainty as to whether the style originated from Tunisia. A theory gives credence to individuals who have developed this technique as an easy way of producing warmth.

Another theory believes the Tunisian Crochet pattern to be an evolution of merging styles practiced in regions of Africa. A couple of other nations in the tropics were also noted to make good use of the craft. Hooked knitting correlates with crochet and conventional knitting, as its needlework involves running around two long needles with corked ends. Historically, Asia lacks these knitted projects, as North America predates the 1920s.

Textile historians could only trace European examples and the previous models to the mid-years of the nineteenth century. The prefix 'Tunisian' is believed to have first been attached by the French, as they tagged the trendy term 'tricot crochet,' where 'tricot' means 'knitting' in French, thus consolidating Tunisian crochet as a mix of both fabrics.

Ever since the evolution of the Tunisian crochet into the needlework industry, several attractive and awkward names have been attributed to it, including the Russian projects. They include Crochet knits, Tunis Crochets, Shepherd-styled knits, fool's or idiot's stitch, and the railway stitch. The latter technique probably originates from the working-class English girls. In the nineteenth century, these girls were seen spinning their needles through pieces of fabric and wool as they awaited the steam vehicles that'd convey them to the mills and factories where they worked.

Over the years, the popularity of the Tunisian crochet culminated and unlike knitting and conventional crochet, it hasn't yet regained the prevalence it amassed in the nineteenth century. In the English Victorian Era, all varieties of Crochet techniques were practiced. Improved equipment like the sewing wheels afforded the females more hours to pursue profitable leisure activities. At that time, crocheting was of great use and a fascinating attraction to the women of the different societal ilk.

The opportunity even became more promising since the yarn was cheaper than cotton but without as much silky texture as the fine wools and silks. Yarns worked for almost anything, ranging through options like socks, inner fabric laces, delicate collars, and fancy tablecloths, amongst others. Due to the sudden rise in the aspect of book publishing, nineteenth-century publishers took advantage of the rising awareness of the people regarding yarns. Then, they started creating detailed manual guides.

In 1907, one very useful guide was made, and the introduction reads as follows; Working with the most basic styles involves utilizing techniques like the dolt stitch lines, tricot stitch lines, and others. These techniques work efficiently for projects like rugs and other materials requiring that the miniature squares be sewn closely. The book also explained that the supposed styles were inadequate for fabric strips of a very light nature and feel. In some cold tropical areas, these styles have been great for the birth of sweaters and neck shawls.

The Tunisian crochet craft remained bright and shiny until 1920 when it suffered a massive decline. At first, the issue of people quickly losing interest was raised. In the early twenties, the tales of the declining interest took an even deeper and sadder twist as women had little to no interest in the craft. Within the 1970s, restoration was brought back to the craft, especially in the U.S. Indeed, most practicing crafters remained ignorant of the assortment of patterns accessible to them, generally utilizing the fundamental stitches in most of the projects. Consequent enhancements of the very basic designs stood as the perfect base for weaving and cross-stitching.

Tunisian Crochet Vs. Traditional Crochet

There have been misconceptions about the 'Tunisian Crochet' and the 'Traditional Crochet.' While it's true that Tunisian crochet is sold as an additional skill to the traditional crochet, there are differences between them. We shall consider three (3) major differences between them:

1. The tools: Traditional crochet uses a hook that's typically around 6" long. The hook has a straight end on one side of the crochet and at the other end. Different materials such as aluminum, plastic, or wood were used in constructing the handle. The handle provides comfort and prevents fatigue and injury on the craftsman or craftswoman.

The Tunisian Crochet hook, on the other hand, comes in sizes ranging from 11" to 14". It's usually not designed with thumb rest; however, it is designed with a knobbed end that ensures the stitches do not fall off. It looks more like a knitting needle with a crochet hook head and a smooth shaft that runs along the handles.

2. The construction: The traditional crochet follows the principle of "one stitch at a time." Fundamentally, that means that you will need to complete one stitch for most of the patterns before making the next stitch. When you get to the end of a row, upturn your work, make continuous chains, and ensure the pattern is continued down the row.

   Unlike the traditional crochet, Tunisian crochet requires during the forward pass for the stitches to be worked onto the hook, then for the return pass that it be worked off the hook. Remember that Tunisian crochet is usually done on the project's front or right side. Because of the stitches amassed on the hook, the forward pass feels similar to knitting when worked on. The stitches are deemed "live" after the return pass is completed until they are worked with additional stitches or are bound off.

Tunisian stitches differ from knitting stitches in that the stitches below them are not supported. This means that in Tunisian crochet, if you drop a stitch, you can simply retrieve or rectify it by pulling out just a row.

3. The fabric: Beginners will be unable to differentiate between the fabrics of Tunisian and conventional crochet. Not to mention that a few tend to mix up Tunisian crochet with weaving or knitting. In reality, however, the main difference in both types of crochet is the fabric produced by both techniques.

For instance, if swatches of Tunisian and traditional crochet are made using similar yarns and hook size, several differences in the result will be observed as given below:

- Stretch: Several stretches exist in all directions for traditional crochet fabric. The fabric hardly creates a stretch horizontally because of the bars the return pass produces; however, several stretches exist vertically. And as a result, traditional crochet fabric hardly bounces back compared to Tunisian crochet.

- Edges: The fabric of Tunisian crochet comes so naturally, with well-arranged borders on the individual fabric's edge. Similar to conventional crochet stitches tops, continuous V's are also produced when the stitches in the first and last row are constructed, thereby creating a fine outlook in Tunisian crochet fabric, bringing together strips of fabric and also in the addition of borders.

Chapter 2

Tunisian Crochet Tips and Tricks

As already mentioned, Tunisian crochet is a technique arising from the mix of knitting and crochet, thus making the best of both needlework techniques. Like crochet, Tunisian crochet also has a hook but is very long, similar to straight knitting needles, or with an attached cord similar to circular knitting needles. The rows in Tunisian crochet are made up of a forward and return pass, creating a lovely textured fabric. However, learning something new comes with the possibility of running into a couple of hitches, hence the need to learn the tips and tricks of the trade. This section focuses on a few of the important tips and tricks that could help your start right on your journey toward making beautifully crafted Tunisian crochet projects. Let's check them out.

1. Increase the hook size

For knitting and crocheting, an estimated size of the hook/needle is given to you when you purchase yarn. But when it comes to Tunisian crochet, the hook size will not generally translate as the former. For the fabric to have a little drape and not be rigid, increase it up at least 1-2 millimeters from what you'd normally use for other needlework. With a Tunisian crochet hook of 8mm, you are good to go for your first buy, given it can be used for several weights of yarn.

2. Count the loops.

It can be difficult for a newbie in Tunisian crochet to ensure they correctly work on the number of stitches on each row. Just like beginners in crocheting, who produced a triangle rather than a blanket or scarf, newbies in Tunisian crochet could also make a couple of funny mistakes. To minimize your mistakes, ensure the number of loops on your hook is counted prior to completing the return pass. And that's easier than counting stitches!

3. Pull on your work

When learning Tunisian, identifying the legs of the arches can be challenging. They can be lost in the process, especially if a smaller hook is used. Don't be scared of pulling up on your work so you can identify these stitches more clearly. Because you'll be working into these legs when you work on your forward pass, it's critical that you are able to see them.

4. Acknowledge the curl and block

One of the predominant challenges in Tunisian crochet is curly edges, notably in Tunisian Simple Stitch. This can be addressed when you increase the hook size, nevertheless, note that this action may alter your fabric's total drape and even make it looser. To avoid this issue altogether, simply ensure your piece is blocked. Block per the fiber's content; this will take care of the curl edges. Some Tunisian crocheters may prefer to acknowledge and use the curly edges as a fashion statement on the edges of their fabric.

5. Yarn consumption

That is correct. Tunisian crochet, unlike knitting and crochet, uses a lot of yarn. The texture that you may achieve in the fabric, on the other hand, cannot be compared to either craft. Although it bears a close resemblance to both, its technique is quite different, and it should be treated as such because it will consume the quantity of yarn it needs; however, you'll be pleased with the outcome.

6. Count the number of stitches you have on your hook

Given how Tunisian crochet works, the back bar and the loop's two legs being worked into could confuse you. As a result, it's easier for your stitches to be counted while they're still on your hook before finishing your return pass. This is the easiest and closest way stitches are counted when knitting rather than attempting to decipher the part of the stitch to count after your return pass.

7. No 'Turning the Work'

Keep in mind that the individual row doesn't just consist of one part; rather, each is made up of two parts. The first is the forward pass (worked from the right side to the left side if you are right-handed) and the second is the reverse pass (worked from the left side to the right side). In the forward pass, you are to pick up your loops, holding it on your hook, while in the reverse pass, the stitches are to be worked back off the loop, meaning no "turning the work" when making Tunisian crochet.

8. Know how to use the vertical bars

In Tunisian crochet, when the forward pass is worked on, the first vertical bar is to be skipped. Then, ensure that the loops always start with the second vertical bar. An error in this process may not turn out well for you.

9. Watching your tension

You must watch your tension because when your Tunisian Crochet work is very tight, it will lead to curled work. Just see to it that your work is not too tight to avoid this from happening.

10. Use stitch markers

While working on your Tunisian crochet, keep in mind that loops are held on your hook, similar to knitting, and this implies that laying down your work mid-row to attend to other pressing issues could cause your loops to fall off and your work to unravel. To avoid this, use stitch markers anytime you want to take a break so that it's easy to identify the spot you stopped at upon resumption of your Tunisian crochet work.

Chapter 3

Getting Started With Tunisian Crochet

Tools and Materials of the Trade

Tunisian Crochet Hook

By now, you should have known that the most special tool you will be needing in making Tunisian crochet projects is the Tunisian crochet hook. However, you could make smaller projects or practice using the regular crochet hook without a handle. Tunisian crochet comes in three different types, which we will look into subsequently. You can give each type a try to help you figure out which is comfortable the most for you.

Long Tunisian Hook

The long Tunisian crochet hooks are made from aluminum and usually come in 10 or 14 inches. This type of hook has on one end a stopper, which prevents your work from sliding off your hook while working on your project

Using the 14-inch hook can be tricky; that is, if you sit on a chair that has arms or you sit at the end of a couch and you're not careful, the end of the hook could hit the arm of the chair, so you need to be mindful of this. Although the 14-inch hook are heavy, they are ideal for beginners since they are generally inexpensive and easy to come by.

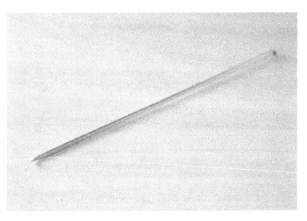

Tunisian Crochet Hook With Extension Cord

The next common hook is the Tunisian crochet hook that has an extension cord attached to one of its ends. It has two kinds; one whose end has a cord and a stopper that is attached permanently to it and the other that can be interchanged.

You can quickly screw your cord to the hook's end per the size you prefer using and then also screw the stopper to the extension cord's end.

This type of hook is manufactured using bamboo or plastic material and is also light in weight. Bear in mind that an interchangeable hook is a great investment if you intend to be an expert Tunisian crocheter.

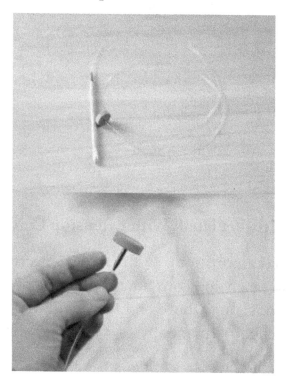

Double-Ended Tunisian Crochet Hook

This is the next common hook in the Tunisian crochet hook family. They are great when you need to work on Tunisian crochet projects in the round. Although this type of hook can be used to work flat Tunisian crochet projects, you will have to attach a rubber band or tape to the hook's end to prevent the stitches from sliding off the hook.

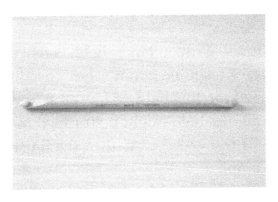

Yarn

Tunisian crochet does not necessitate the use of any unique yarn. Some yarns, however, are better suited to this sort of crochet compared to others. For example, novelty yarn with a lot of fur or a lot of bobbles isn't appropriate for Tunisian crochet because you will be unable to see the stitches, or the tension will not be consistent all through the pattern.

Wool yarn and simple yarn made from natural fibers such as cotton and bamboo will be suited for Tunisian crochet's thicker fabric. A merino wool yarn provides not just a fabric that is both soft and flexible with an excellent stitch definition but will also give you an amazing texture and feel. You'll realize the true beauty of Tunisian crochet when your stitches are well defined.

However, fibers with a large halo, such as Rowan's Kidsilk Haze, should not be used. This is because instead of the halo to lay atop the work like when you knit, the halo might be trapped in the stitches (same as fur yarn), with the finished work looking unkempt.

If you don't want to use animal fibers, try natural plant fibers such as bamboo, acrylics and cotton or mixes of synthetic-natural fiber such as Stylecraft, Lion Brand and Rowan.

Although silk fiber or silk mixes are incredibly delightful to hold and touch, they are rarely used in Tunisian crochet due to the vast amount of yarn required in making an afghan, clothing item, or adornment such as a scarf. If you want to use a silk mix, a little clutch purse might be the way to go.

25

Standard Crochet Materials

The only special tool you need to start with is the Tunisian crochet hook, especially if you are not new to crocheting. Other crocheting tools to get before you start include:

Scissors
Small sharp scissors are invaluable for cutting yarn whenever necessary

Tapestry Needle
The wool tapestry needle is used for weaving in ends and binding pieces together. Wool tapestry needles with a large eye and fairly blunt point are the best.

Stitch Markers
Marking tools define stitches such as the start or end of a short row, a pattern repeat, or stitch positioning.

Tape Measure
The tape measure is indispensable for checking measurements all through the process of the Crochet piece.

Row Counters

Remember, 2 rows; the Forward and the Standard Return Pass, define a single row in Tunisian crochet

Blocking Board and Pins

The interconnecting foam boards found in hardware stores or toy shops are the best tools for blocking boards. Tunisian crochet tends to curl, and blocking is an essential process to ensure a nice flat piece of work or fabric. Pins help you to hold down your work when blocking. You must ensure they are rust-free so you don't stain your work.

Tunisian Crochet Symbols, Charts, and Abbreviations

Note: This book assumes that you have some prior knowledge of crochet. If you are not familiar with some of the concepts discussed in this book, then it's important to lay your hands on some online crocheting tutorials as you progress with the rest of this book's content.

Tunisian Crochet Symbols

Years ago, Japan developed the standardized Tunisian crochet symbols that have significantly aided the Tunisian crochet craft. However, several other

crocheters worldwide have developed their own standard symbols. To the best of my knowledge, only Japan so far has an official standard symbol for knitting and crocheting that publishers are obligated to comply with by law.

So in this section, you will be learning various chart symbols that you will encounter as a crocheter.

Below is a sample chart comparable to what is obtainable in a Japanese pattern book:

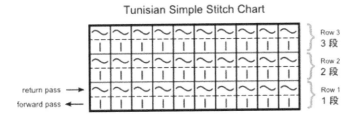

Because there are 10 stitches per row on this chart, you will work the forward pass by dragging the yarn via the individual chain's back bump, skipping the first chain, and finishing with 10 loops on your hook. Some patterns may advise you to maintain the first chain and not to skip it; in that case, you will have just chain 9 at the start; this will give you a rounder corner, but it's unadvisable if you will seam later on.

Color Key:

White = Japanese symbols (basic ones are standard)

Sky blue = Symbols from The Harmony Guide to Crochet Stitches

Gold = Symbols from Renate Kirkpatrick's Crochet Techniques (U.K. terminology)

Plum = Symbols from Donna Kooler's Encyclopedia of Crochet

Notes:

- Begin with yarn in the back unless otherwise stipulated.

- Except otherwise specified, "slide the hook into the vertical bar," meaning from right to left.

- Except otherwise specified, yarn overs are worked back to front over the top of the hook. For reverse-based stitches like Purl Stitch, Japanese pattern books often employ a Reverse yarn over, but American pattern books use the standard yarn over. The reverse yarn overs are

used to make double-sided stitch patterns with exact similarities on each side.

- There is a naming dispute between Reverse and Purl. The fact that Slip Stitch refers to two separate stitches adds to the confusion (one with crochet origin, the other with knit origin).

Symbol Chart

SYMBOL	TUNISIAN STITCH NAMES	DESCRIPTION
	Chain Stitch, 鎖編み目 *kusari amime*	Yarn over, pull yarn through loop on hook.
	Simple Stitch (Tss), loop or knit stitch, simple or Afghan stitch, 表編み目 *omote amime*	Insert hook into vertical bar, yarn over, pull yarn through bar.
	Return Stitch (R), Return Chain, もどり編み目 *modori amime*	Yarn over, pull yarn through next two loops on hook, except for the first stitch of the row in which the yarn is pulled through only one loop.
	Bind Off, Crochet Slip Stitch, Tricot slip stitch, slip stitch, 引抜き編み目 *hikinuki amime*	Insert hook into vertical bar from right to left, yarn over, pull yarn through bar and loop on hook.
	Purl Stitch (Tps), 裏編み目 *ura amime*	Bring yarn to front, insert hook into vertical bar, yarn over [reverse yarn over], pull yarn through bar. This stitch is sometimes referred as Reverse Stitch in some publications.

31

Slip Stitch with yarn in front, 浮き目 *ukime* — With yarn held in front, insert hook into vertical bar.

 Twisted Stitch, Twisted Tunisian simple stitch (TwTss), twisted knit, ねじり編み目 *nejiri amime* — Insert hook into vertical bar from left to right, yarn over, pull yarn through loop.

 Reverse Twisted Stitch, twisted purl, 裏ねじり編み目 *ura nejiri amime* — With yarn held in front, insert hook into vertical bar from left to right, yarn over [reverse yarn over], pull yarn through loop.

 3-in-1 Stitch Increase, 3目の編み出し増し目 *amidashi mashime* — Insert hook into vertical bar, yarn over, pull yarn through bar, yarn over, insert hook into same vertical bar, yarn over, pull yarn through bar.

 2-to-1 Stitch Decrease – forward pass, Tunisian simple stitch two together (Tss2tog), loop under two vertical bars, 2目一度 *nime ichido* — Insert hook into two vertical bars, yarn over, pull yarn through both bars.

Reverse Stitch (Trs),
Back Loop Stitch,
Tss worked into back
loop only of stitch in
previous row,
すじ編み目
suji amime
バックステッチ
*bakku sutecchi (back
stitch)*

Move the Return chain
to front, insert hook
into vertical bar on
back side, yarn over,
pull yarn through bar.
(Alt. description: Tss
behind the Return
chain.)

 Knit Stitch (Tks),
stocking stitch,
メリヤス編み目
meriyasu amime

Insert hook into front
of loop below the
Return chain, yarn over,
pull yarn through loop.

Reverse Knit Stitch,
裏メリヤス編み目
*ura meriyasu amime
(Purl Stitch from
knitting)*

With yarn held in front,
insert hook through
back of loop below the
Return chain, yarn over
[reverse yarn over], pull
yarn through loop.

Yarn Over,
increase one Tunisian
simple stitch (Inc 1
Tss),
かけ目
kakeme

Yarn over the hook,
back to front.

Reverse Yarn Over,
手前かけ目
temae kakeme

Yarn over the hook,
front to back.

 Tunisian Slip Stitch
(Tsl),
Tunisian slipped
stitch (Tsl st),
すべり目
suberime

Insert hook into
vertical bar.

33

⼊	3-to-1 Stitch Decrease – forward pass, **Tunisian simple stitch three together (Tss3tog),** 3目一度 sanme ichido	Insert hook into three vertical bars, yarn over, pull yarn through all three bars
丁 下	2-to-1 Stitch Decrease – return pass, もどり2目一度 modori nime ichido	Yarn over, pull yarn through next three loops on hook.
朩	3-to-1 Stitch Decrease – return pass, もどり3目一度 modori sanme ichido	Yarn over, pull yarn through next four loops on hook.
† T † †	Double Crochet (Tdc), **Tunisian half double crochet (Thdc), treble (tr), incomplete double crochet,** 長編み目 naga amime	This is worked the same as a regular double crochet stitch, except for leaving the last loop on the hook.
† † † †	Treble Crochet (Ttr), **Tunisian double crochet (Tdc), double treble (dtr), incomplete treble crochet,** 長々編み目 naga naga amime	This is worked the same as a regular treble crochet stitch, except for leaving the last loop on the hook.

Common Tunisian Crochet Abbreviations

The following is a cross-section of some common regular crochet and Tunisian crochet abbreviations that you will encounter throughout the rest of this book.

Abbreviation	Description
etss	extended Tunisian simple stitch
FwP	forward pass
RetP	return pass
tdc	Tunisian double crochet
tfs	Tunisian full stitch
thdc	Tunisian half double crochet
tks	Tunisian knit stitch
tps	Tunisian purl stitch
trs	Tunisian reverse stitch
tsc	Tunisian single crochet
tss	Tunisian simple stitch
TssBL	Tunisian Simple Stitch in the Back Loop
tslst	Tunisian slip stitch
ttr	Tunisian treble crochet
ttw	Tunisian twisted
ch	chain stitch
lp	Loop
MC	main color
rep	Repeat
sc	single crochet
sk	Skip
sl st	slip stitch
st	Stitch
yo	yarn over
Hk	Hook
*	Repeat the instructions following the single asterisk

Structure of a Tunisian Crochet Stitch

Creating several Tunisian crochet stitches depends on the location your hook is inserted. To grasp hook insertion, you need to understand the various components that make up a stitch, as given below:

Horizontal bar: This is the topmost part of the stitch. For regular crochet stitches, this part is where your hook is normally inserted.

Front and back vertical bars: Tunisian stitches normally have 2 vertical bars: the closet one to you in the front and the one that's farthest from you in the back

Space between stitches: This space sits between one set and the next set of the front and back vertical bars

Basic Tunisian Crochet Stitches

In this section, we will focus on learning about the common Tunisian crochet stitches, but let's start with the basics!

Keep in mind that each Tunisian crochet row is made up of a forward and a reverse pass. Pick up loops from the row below and leave them on your hook while working from the right side to the left. This gives you a forward pass.

Once you are done with all the stitches from the previous row, the return pass is worked on to finish your row. Yarn over, pulling through a few loops until you reach the end; this marks the end of the return pass.

Setup or Foundation Row:

Tunisian crochet stitches or projects begin with a setup or foundation row; know this before making your first stitch.

To start, select a yarn and a hook whose size is at least two times more than what was suggested in the yarn label. Most hooks typically provide space for 10 stitches on the neck. Otherwise, just follow the guide below to make fewer chains.

1. Chain row: Form a slip stitch, inserting your hook right into it.

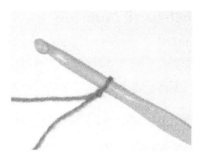

Make a foundation by crocheting 9 chains. This
will result in 10 stitches because your hook's loop
has a total of 10.

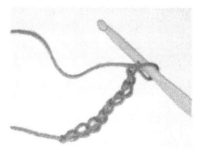

Upturn your work to the side for a clearer view of
the bumps that are normally visible behind your
work. This will give you the loops to insert your
hook.

2. Forward Pass (Pick up loops): The first bump is right beside your hook; slide your hook into that bump. Others may choose to skip this bump which becomes challenging to hook into. If this works for you, then go for it.

Yarn over, pulling through 1 loop. At this moment, there are 2 loops on your hook.

*Slide your hook into the subsequent bump, yarn over, pulling through only 1 loop

*Repeat until all bumps have been used up. There will be 10 loops on your hook on getting to the end.

3. Return Pass (Finish each stitch): Chain 1; Yarn over, pulling through only 1 loop (this is your work's left edge/ side)

Yarn over, pulling through 2 loops. Repeat until there is just 1 loop left on your hook.

Note: Don't pull tight, especially with just 1 loop left on your hook. Tightening your work so hard will make it challenging to continue with a good result.

And that's just about it. You are now set for your next row. This is where you now apply the basic Tunisian crochet stitches, and that's what we will be looking at in subsequent sections

Tunisian Simple Stitch (TSS)

The Tunisian simple stitch is one of the most basic stitches every beginner must get the hang of when starting Tunisian crochet. It's such a delight to practice.

Here is how to make this type of stitch:

1. Skip the row's first stitch

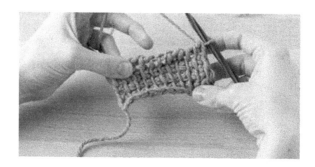

2. Slide in your hook starting from the right side to the left just beneath the front vertical bar

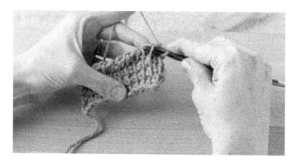

3. Yarn over, pulling 1 loop up

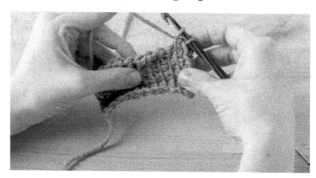

4. The loop should be left on the hook, then proceed across the row

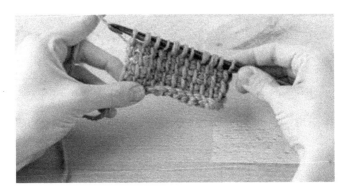

5. Return pass: Yarn over, pulling across 1 loop

6. *Yarn over, pulling across 2 loops

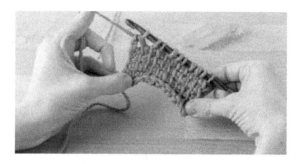

7. Repeat from * until your hook has 1 loop left

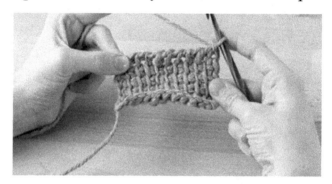

Tunisian Knit Stitch (TKS)

This type of Tunisian crochet stitch creates stitches that closely resemble the knit stitches; no wonder its name.

Here is how to make this type of stitch:

1. Skip the row's first stitch

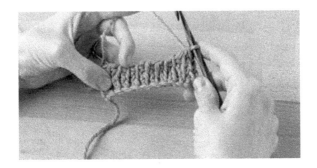

2. Slide in your hook in-between the front and back vertical bar

3. Yarn over, pulling 1 loop up

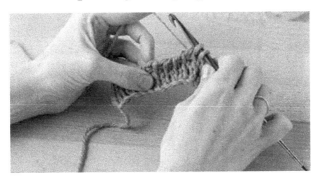

4. The loop should be left on the hook, then proceed across the row

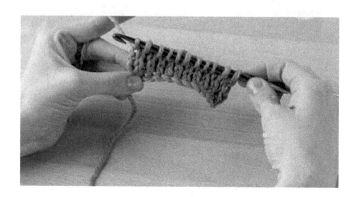

5. Return pass: Yarn over, pulling across 1 loop

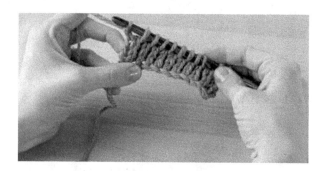

6. *Yarn over, pulling across 2 loops

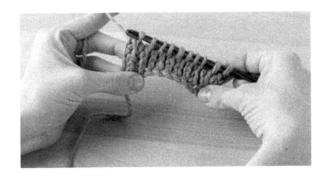

7. Repeat from * until your hook has 1 loop left

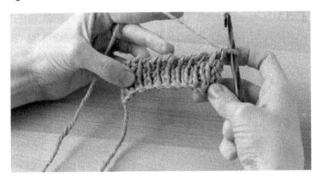

Tunisian Purl Stitch (TPS)

This stitch closely resemble the process and attributes of the purl stitch when you are knitting

Here is how to make this type of stitch:

1. Skip the row's first stitch

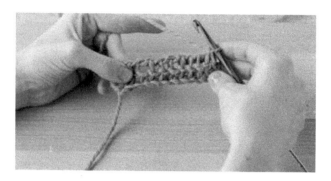

2. The yarn should be taken to the front of the work, then slide in the hook starting from right to left across the front vertical bar

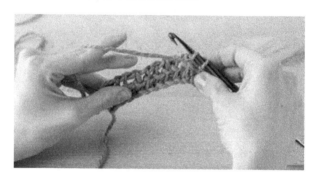

3. Yarn over, pulling 1 loop up

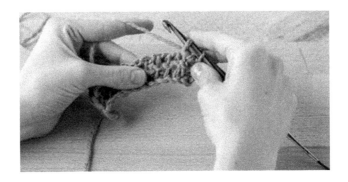

4. The loop should be left on the hook, then proceed across the row

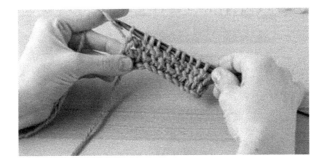

5. Return pass: Yarn over, pulling across 1 loop

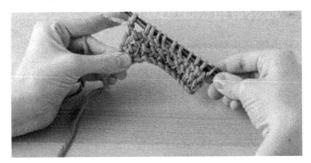

6. *Yarn over, pulling across 2 loops

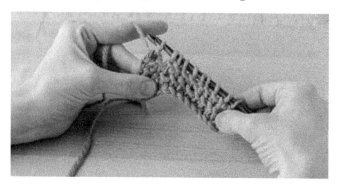

7. Repeat from * until your hook has 1 loop left

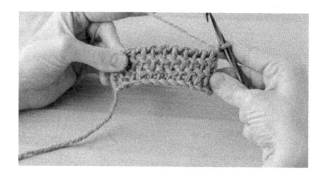

Tunisian Reverse Stitch (TRS)

These kinds of stitches are excellent when you want to infuse texture into your Tunisian crochet projects.

1. Skip the row's first stitch

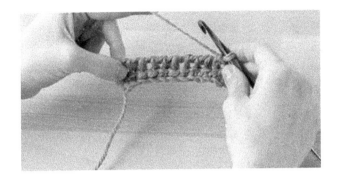

2. Slide in the hook starting from the right to the left below the back vertical bar

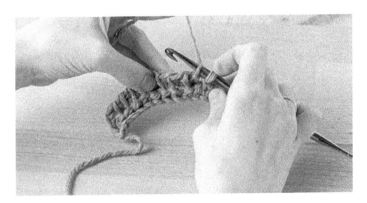

3. Yarn over, pulling 1 loop up

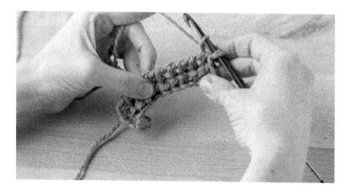

4. The loop should be left on the hook, then proceed across the row

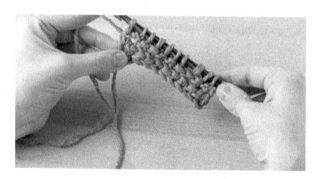

5. Return pass: Yarn over, pulling across 1 loop

6. *Yarn over, pulling across 2 loops

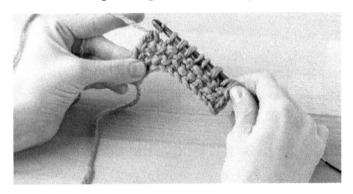

7. Repeat from * until your hook has 1 loop left

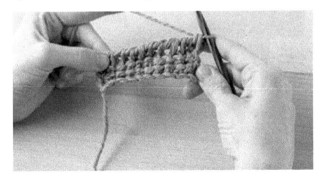

Tunisian Full Stitch (TFS)

This s very easy to make with a distinct look compared to other stitches.

Here is how to make this type of stitch:

1. Skip the row's first stitch

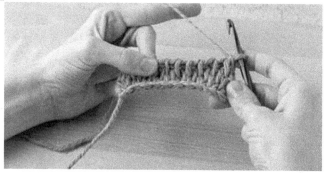

2. Slide in the hook below the horizontal bar in the gap/ space between stitches

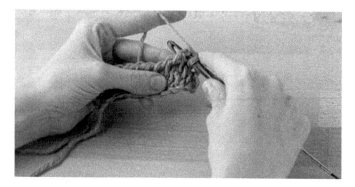

3. Yarn over, pulling 1 loop up

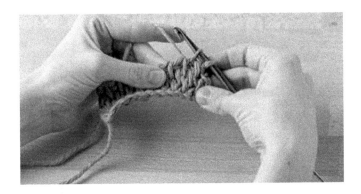

4. The loop should be left on the hook, then proceed across the row

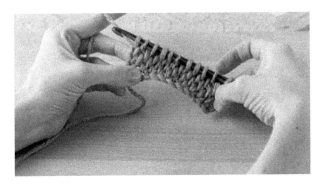

5. Return pass: Yarn over, pulling across 1 loop

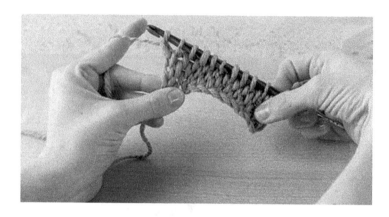

6. *Yarn over, pulling across 2 loops

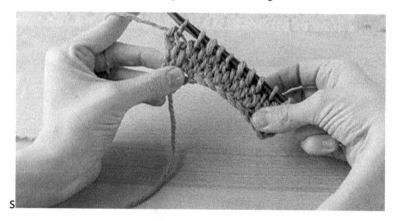

7. Repeat from * until your hook has 1 loop left

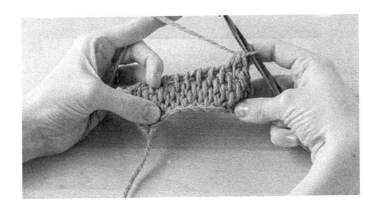

Binding Off a Tunisian Crochet

Like knitting, a bind-off row is needed in Tunisian crochet in securing ongoing stitches to give a nice finished edge.

In Tunisian crochet, the bind off is identical to how slip stitches are worked in traditional crochet. Slide in your hook below the next vertical bar for a simple stitch bind off. Yarn over, pulling a loop across the two vertical bars and the loop on the hook. See demonstration below;

This gives you one stitch that you have worked on.
Proceed until you get to the last stitch.

Tunisian Crochet Color Change

Colorwork addition to a Tunisian project crochet can be
as easy as adding a unique stripe of color to a pattern.

It could also be as complex as required in describing a lovely snowflake or some other object. You can likewise use the return pass in making changes to your colors, which can add an intriguing touch to your project.

Color change can be added to a Tunisian crochet project in several ways and below, we will be discussing the different ways you can switch up your project with color addition.

1. **Changing colors at the start of a row**

For colors to be changed at the start of a row, colors will first need to be changed at the end of the return pass before the row you want to change the color on.

On getting to the end of the row of the color currently being used, perform a return pass until your hook has 2 loops left on it, yarn over using the new color (dropping the old color), pulling across the 2 loops on the hook.

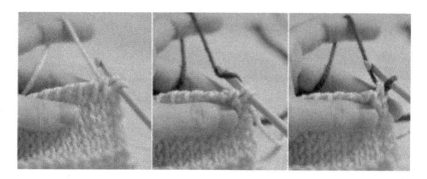

Slide the hook into the stitch to be made (the stitch used here is the Tunisian knit stitch), and with the new yarn, pull a loop up.

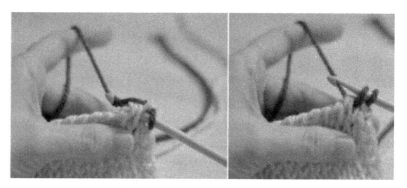

2. Changing colors in the middle of a row

If your project has a fair isle or intarsia design, color change in the middle of a row can be helpful.

To change colors in the subsequent stitch, simply slide the hook into your desired stitch (the stitch used here is the Tunisian knit stitch), yarn over using the new color (dropping the old color), and with the new color, pull a loop up.

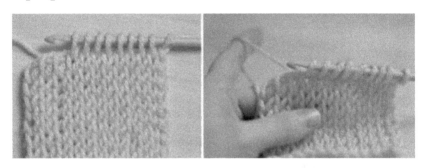

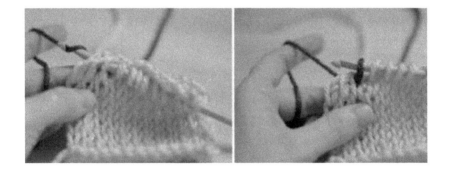

3. Changing colors in the return pass

Upon changing colors in the forward pass, the color change will also have to be made in the return pass, except stated otherwise by the pattern. The example below is a forward pass with just one color change.

Now, perform the return pass as you normally do until the new and old colors are on the right and left side, respectively, then use the new color to yarn over (dropping the old color), pulling through your hook's the first 2 loops.

The new and old colors are on the left and right sides, respectively. With the old color (dropping the new color), yarn over, pulling through your hook's first 2 loops, and proceed with the row.

4. Changing colors at the start of the return pass

Color change at the start of a return pass can give your project a lovely look and can make your work have a marled look, especially if you use the Tunisian simple stitch.

Create a chain using a single color of yarn, then for the first row, make a forward pass.

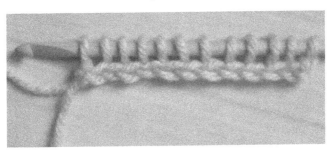

Upon pulling a loop up at the end of the chain, use the new color (dropping the old one) to yarn over, pulling through your hook's first loop.

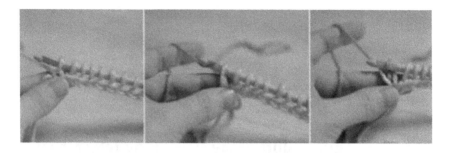

Proceed with the return pass, yarn over, and pull 2 loops through until your hook has 1 loop left on it

Use the new yarn to finish the forward pass with your preferred stitch (the stitch used here is the Tunisian simple stitch). Use the new yarn to yarn over, and finish the return pass.

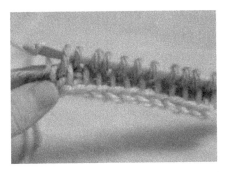

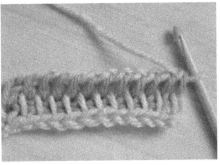

Proceed by changing the yarn at the start of each return pass

Increase and Decrease In Tunisian Crochet

By now, you may think you already have a firm grip on Tunisian crochet and I want to believe so because you will start putting what you have length into actual projects. However, before then, there are a couple of things to be learned to become a PRO even though you are a beginner, and that is how you can increase and decrease in Tunisian crochet.

Inceasing and decresing occur in different ways; however, they occur in the forward pass; the reverse pass is done normally. Below are the known techniques using a Tunisian simple stitch.

How to Increase

1. Yarn Over Method: To make an increase, yarn over, then continue to work the pattern as you would normally do. Slide in your hook below the next vertical bar, then pull a loop up. On your hook, you will see the yarn over appearing as a new loop or stitch.

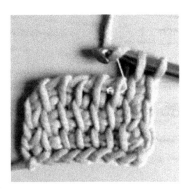 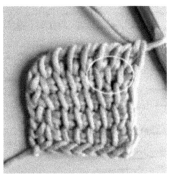

2. Full Stitch Method: To make an increase, slide in your hook in-between the space of your vertical bars, then yarn over, pulling a loop up. Continue to work the pattern as you would normally do.

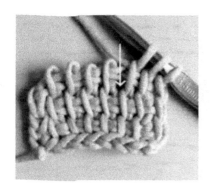
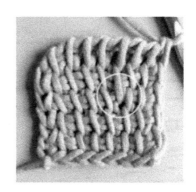

3. Horizontal Bar Method: To make an increase, slide in your hook below a vertical bar and across horizontal bars (the first two) next to it. Yarn over, pulling a loop up, and continue to work only on the same vertical bar, then pull a loop up.

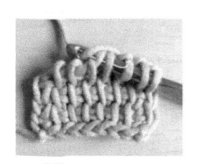

4. Back Bump Method: To make an increase, slide your hook below the back bump (behind the vertical bar to be worked in), yarn over, pulling a loop up. Continue to work on the same vertical

bar (you just finished working in its back bu
as you would normally do.

 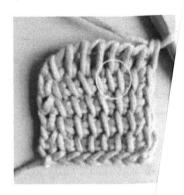

5. Back and Front Bar Method: To make an
    slide your hook (starting from the fro
    back) below a stitch's back bar, bring i
    yarn over, pulling a loop up. Continue
    the same stitch as you would normal
    in your hook below its vertical bar,
    loop up.

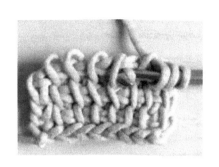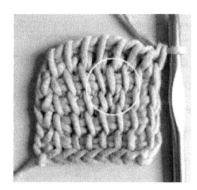

How to Decrease

1. Stitch Skipping Method: To make a decrease, the vertical bar you are to work in should be skipped, then continue to work directly below the next vertical bar; pull a loop up.

2. The 2 Together Method: To make a decrease, slide in your hook below 2 vertical bars together (i.e.,

the vertical bar you are to work in and that just after it), yarn over, pulling a loop up. Continue to work on the remaining stitches as you would normally do

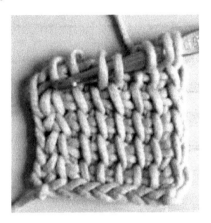

A Short Message From The Author:

Hey, I hope you are enjoying the book? I would love to hear your thoughts!

Many readers do not know how hard reviews are to come by and how much they help an author.

I would be incredibly grateful if you could take just 60 seconds to write a short review on Amazon, even if it is a few sentences!

>> Click here to leave a quick review

Thanks for the time taken to share your thoughts!

Chapter 4

Tunisian Crochet Project Patterns

This chapter details the practical application of all that has been discussed before now. Without much ado, let's get right into it.

Tunisian Crochet Ear Warmer

Materials

- 1 Skein bulky (5) yarn (65 yards approximately)
- 6.5mm straight crochet hook with no handle
- Tapestry needle
- Scissors

Gauge and Measurements

Gauge: 14 sts x 9 rows = 4-inch square.

The completed project has a measurement of 10.5" wide x 4.5" tall when sewn together. The gauge is only necessary for this ear warmer project if you intend to make this project have these exact measurements. If not, you can use your own measurement.

Note: From here on now, we would be making use of abbreviations in most cases, so kindly familiarize yourself with the Tunisian crochet abbreviation table shared earlier.

Instructions

1. Ch 16. Begin with the 2nd chain from your hook and slide your hook into the stitch, yarn over, pulling a loop up. With the loop on the hook, slide your hook into the next chain, pulling another loop up. Proceed with pulling loops up in the individual chain stitch throughout the row.

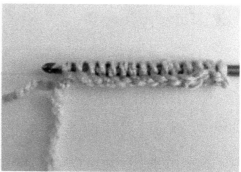

2. Begin your return pass—first, chain 1 with the 1st loop. Yarn over, pulling across 2 loops.

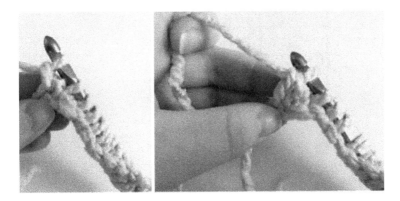

3. Again, yarn over, pulling across another 2 loops. Continue this trend until you arrive at the row's end.

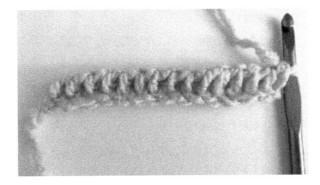

4. Start the forward pass next. This row should be worked into the previous row's vertical loops.

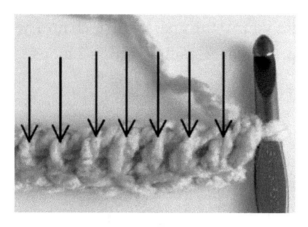

5. Slide your hook into the 2nd vertical loop. Yarn over, pulling a loop up.

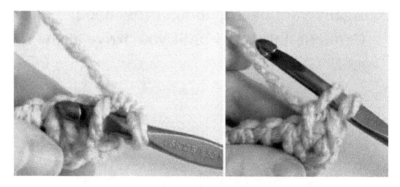

6. Keeping the loop on your hook, your hook should be inserted into the next vertical loop, yarn over, pulling a loop up. Continue in this trend until you arrive at the row's final stitch. For the final stitch, slide your hook into the 2 loops at the row's end. Yarn over, pulling a loop up.

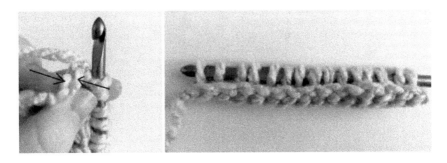

7. Make another return pass. Continue in this trend; forward pass, return pass.

8. Make 51 rows.

9. For the final row, make a slip stitch into the
   individual vertical loop across the row.

10. Tie off and leave a long tail to be sewn later on. Ensure the ends of the ear warmer are folded with the right sides facing in. Lay the two ends side by side, making sure they overlap.

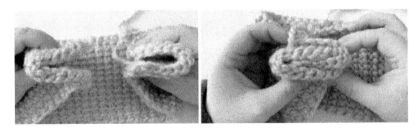

11. Sew this edge together. Ensure the four layers are sewn then, turn your work right side out.

Tunisian Crochet Washcloth

Materials

- Worsted weight yarn in two coordinated colors
- 4mm regular crochet hook
- 6mm Tunisian crochet hook

Note:

- This washcloth has 30 chains and a measurement of 20 cm (without border)
- This project uses the Tunisian simple stitch and should be worked to 29 rows approximately.

Take note, the number of rows is dependent on your yarn. To ensure your washcloth is squared perfectly upon completion, you should check its size by ensuring the bottom right-hand corner is folded diagonally up to the top left-hand corner.

- Once a square is gotten, cast/ bind off

Instructions

Foundation row

1. **Forward Pass**

   - As you would normally, form a chain of your desired length

   - Beginning from the 2nd chain from your hook, slide your hook into your chain's top loop, yarn over, pulling a loop up; leave the loop on your hook

- Proceed in this manner until you arrive at the end; keep the loops on your hook.

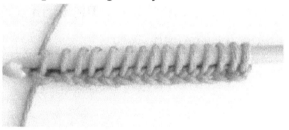

2. Return Pass

Now, we will finish the second part of the row). This step will be applicable for other rows moving forward.

- Work from the left to the right, then yarn over, pulling across 1 loop (only the first stitch)

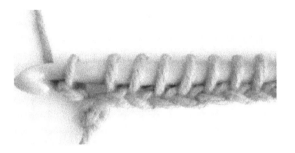

- Yarn over, pulling across 2 loops to end

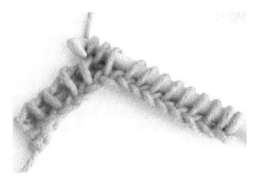

- In the end, a loop would be left on your hook

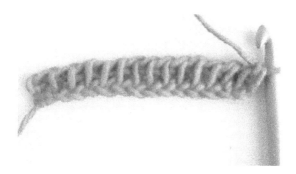

To make a row:

1. **Forward pass**

   - Insert your hook across the 2nd vertical bar from the previous row

   - Yarn over, pulling across 2 loops (your hook now has 2 loops on it)

- Proceed in this same manner, and ensure all loops are kept on your hook until you get to the row's end.

To give your edges a fine look, go through the back of both loops on the last stitch.

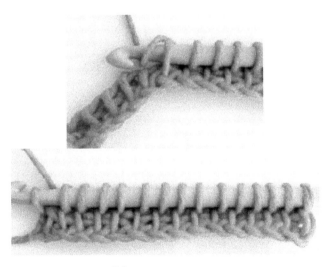

2. Return Pass

- To complete the row, make a return pass, just like in the foundation row above. This will give you the Tunisian simple stitch.

Cast/ Bind Off

1. Beginning on a forward pass, your hook should be inserted into the 2nd vertical bar, then pull a loop up. Then, yarn over, making a slip stitch (this is done when you pull your yarn across the 2 loops on your hook)

2. By now, you will be left with 1 loop on your hook. Proceed across the row and slip stitch the individual stitch until you arrive at the end, then fasten off

This washcloth has no border to it. You can choose to go with this as your final piece or add a border to it and switch up your piece to look more attractive. Your crocheting experience will come in very handy in the next section we will look at, so buckle up.

Linen Stitch Border

At this point, you will make use of your regular crochet hook

Row 1:

- Use a contrast color and make a single crochet into the individual stitch around the washcloth.

- Work [single crochet, chain 1, single crochet] in the individual corner, then use a slip stitch to connect with the first single crochet's top.

Row2:

- Work [single crochet, chain 1, single crochet], then;

- *ch 1, skip 1, and make a single crochet up to the next corner [single crochet, chain 1, single crochet].

- Repeat from* to finish off

- Use a slip stitch to connect with the top of the first single crochet. Break yarn off.

Row 3:

- Connect the main color with any chain space corner, then repeat Row 2; however, you will work your space corner into the previous row's chain space.

- Use a slip stitch to connect with the top of the first single crochet. Break yarn off.

Row 4:

Connect contrast color with any chain space corner, working same as you did in Row 3. Break yarn off, weaving the ends in.

That's all!

Tunisian Crochet Basketweave Pillow

Materials

- D.K. weight yarn, approx. 50 gram (for the front piece, a Scheepjes color crafter with "Urk" color was used and for the back piece, a Scheepjes color crafter with "Barneveld" was used)
- U.S. size 9 (5.5 mm) Tunisian crochet cable hook
- Pillow insert (14" x 14"[35cm x 35cm] pillow was used)
- Yarn/ Tapestry needle
- Scissors

Note: The versatility of this pattern is huge! So, use your preferred needle/ yarn size that is okay by you; however, remember the yardage will differ, and the number of repetitions worked for the individual section may have to be adjusted.

Additional note:

- A forward pass's last stitch is always worked in the same manner irrespectively of the stitch you are using; this will be called the end stitch.
- The first and last stitches are not members of the pattern; work them the same way, always.
- Work in multiples of 5.
- For the pillow's pattern front part, Row 2 and every other row that is even are worked using the return pass.

Special Stitches

The special stitches used in this pattern are;

- Tunisian Simple Stitch (TSS)
- Tunisian Knit Stitch (TKS)
- Tunisian Purl Stitch (TPS)

So ensure you refer to chapter 3 in the section where I discussed the "Basic Tunisian Crochet Stitches."

Instructions

The Front Part of the Pillow

Row 1 (The Foundation Row): ch 55; take a loop from the back bump in the 2nd chain from the hook and in the individual chain to end; all the loops should be left on the hook.

Row 2: Work a return pass

Row 3:

- Work a Tunisian knit stitch (Tks) in the subsequent 4 stitches
- *Work a Tunisian purl stitch (Tps) in the subsequent 5 stitches
- Work a Tks in the subsequent 5 stitches
- Repeat from * to the last 5 stitches
- Work a Tks in the next 4 stitches, then work the end stitch.

Row 5-7: Work in the same manner as Row 3

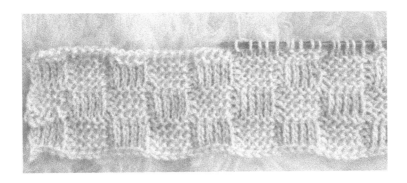

Row 8:

- Work a Tps in the subsequent 4 stitches
- Work a *Tks in the subsequent 5 stitches
- Work a Tps in the subsequent 5 stitches
- Repeat from * to the last 5 stitches
- Work a Tks in the next 4 stitches, then work the end stitch

Row 9-11:

- Work in the same manner as Row 8
- Repeat Rows 3-11 until your piece has a measurement of 14 inches
- Cast/ bind off as you normally would

The Back Part of the Pillow

Row 1 (The Foundation Row): ch 55; take a loop from the back bump in the 2nd chain from the hook and in the individual chain to end; all the loops should be left on the hook.

Row 2: Work a return pass

Row 3:

- Work a Tunisian simple stitch (Tss) to end

- Repeat Rows 2-3 until your piece has a measurement of 14 inches

- Bind off.

Finishing

- With the right sides of your piece together, your piece's long sides and bottom should be sewn using a mattress stitch or a backstitch.

- Insert your pillow and sew to close up.

Tunisian Crochet Coffee Sleeve

The Tunisian knit bow coffee sleeve pattern is a stylish eco-friendly substitute for the paper coffee sleeve. This easy crochet pattern is suitable for beginners wanting to try Tunisian crochet. This pattern uses the regular 10mm crochet hook and only 1/2 an ounce of Bernat Maker Home Dec Yarn for its crocheting.

The 'Bernat Maker Home Dec Yarn' was chosen because the stitch definition of the yarn is second to none and it provides a functional finish and is durable and perfect for everyday use. Also, it could prove difficult to find this yarn in stores, but it can be gotten from Amazon and eBay.

For crochet hooks to use, a 10mm hook with a straight shaft will suffice to help maintain a consistent stitch height.

Materials

- Bernat Maker Home Dec Yarn (0.5 ounces)
- Yarn/ Tapestry Needle
- Stitch Markers
- Scissors
- 10 mm Tunisian crochet hook (with a straight shaft)

Note:

- Always maintain consistency in tension throughout your work (some parts shouldn't be too tight or too loose). It will be good if the final row has a freer tension to make the assembly easier.

- The first loop of the hook at the start of the row, counts as your first stitch. If you intend to use your coffee sleeve for a large cup size (i.e., Starbucks, Venti) then, it's best to start with a Chain 10 so that your sleeve can be taller (3").

- Finished size – Measured when laid flat and well-assembled is 4" (w) x 2.5" (h): 0.5 oz.

- Gauge: 4″ wide = 13 rows and 2.5″ height = 8 stitches

Instructions

Return Pass: This will be the same for the individual row

- Chain 1 by yarning over and pull across 1 loop
- Then *yarn over, pulling across 2 loops
- Repeat* until you have just 1 loop on your hook

Note: The instructions below apply to the forward pass; the return pass as described above remains the same for the individual row.

Row 1:

- Ch 8; turn this chain over, then beginning in the 2nd chain from your hook, pull a loop up in each chain's (ch 8) back bump

(The 1st picture from the left displays the back bump and the 2nd picture displays the loops pulled up on the hook)

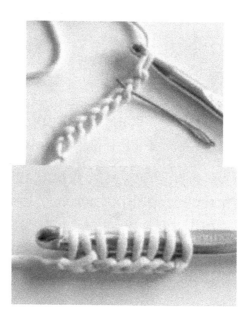

Rows 2 – 28:

- Work across a Tks until you get to the last stitch, then slide your hook below the 2 loops on the stitch's (8) side

  (The 1st picture from the left describe where to slide in your hook to work the Tks, while the 2nd and 3rd

pictures describe where to slide in your hook for the last stitch)

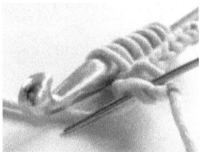
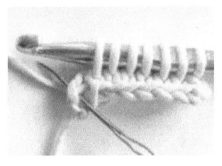

Upon completing Row 28, cut your yarn leaving a 5-inch tail, then tie your project off. You should have a flat panel project measuring 8.5" (w) x 2.5" (h).

Assembling The Coffee Sleeve

Kindly ignore the different colors in yarns from what you have above, it all comes down to the same final piece.

- Flip over your flat panel, and assemble the wrong side out.
- Fold (towards the right side) into half the two ends.
- Then slide into each other the two sides, as shown below

- Using stitch marker(s), both pieces should be held together, as shown below

- Use your needle to stitch the pieces together; ensure all the four layers are picked up, as shown below

- Tie off but just before that, turn your piece to the right side out after stitching to ensure all stitches were picked up.

- After you tie off, weave the tail into a seam to hold in place and to cut loose ends

There you go, the completed right side out coffee sleeve

Tunisian Crochet Cowl

Cowls made from Tunisian styles are excellent projects any beginner or even experts can embark on. It is worked flat and has no increases.

It uses two styles of stitching; the Tunisian knit stitch and the Tunisian purl stitch. This stunning and simple cowl border is made with Tunisian purl stitches, thus making this piece have no curl at the bottom, meaning it does not need blocking unless you feel like it. The yarn used is made from Merino wool and nylon, making it have a very luxurious feel.

Materials

- 3 skeins of Furls Whims Merino Medium Weight Yarn of approx. 280g
- Scissors
- Darning needle
- Measuring tape (optional)
- 12-inch Tunisian crochet hook

Size of Cowl: 22-inch circumference and 12.5-inch tall

- This size can be readily adjusted (see notes)

Gauge: 14 stitches in Tks and 14 rows = 4 inches

- Although gauge is mentioned as given above, there are useful measurements in this course of this pattern construction.

Gauge Tips and Tension

- To get the actual gauge, the recommended hook size should be used
- Ensure that you pull up on the loops during the forward pass to get the right gauge height.

Notes:

- This cowl pattern is worked flat, with the right side facing you.
- At the start of each row is the first stitch on your hook, thus counting as a Tunisian knit stitch.
- Don't turn your piece at the start of the individual row; the individual row is worked in a forward pass (from the right side to the left), then worked in a return pass (from the left side to the right).
- After the cowl is seamed, its circumference will be a little smaller.
- This cowl has a gauge; however, you will come across useful measurements in the course of this pattern.

- You can adjust the size of your cowl when you add several stitches as required to get the right circumference and extra rows to get a taller cowl
- Seam the back of this cowl to finish it off.

Working Into The Row's Last Stitch

- Bring your work closer to you and search for the end of the row's last 2 vertical bars

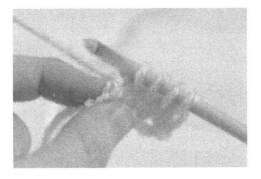

- Slide your hook below the last 2 vertical bars

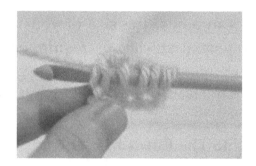

- Yarn over

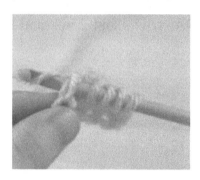

- Pull a loop up

Rows Where Colors Were Changed

- Row 1-15: Skein #1
  After Row 15, your cowl should have an approximate measurement of 4.5" tall.
- Row 16-30: Skein #2
  After Row 30, your cowl should have an approximate measurement of 8.5" tall.
- Row 31-the end: Skein #3
  After Row 41, your cowl should have an approximate measurement of 12" tall.

Changing Colors At The Row's End

- The color change should be made when working the return pass of the final/ last row where you'd prefer the particular color of yarn.
- When your hook has 2 loops left, as shown in the 1st image from the left below, drop the yarn you are currently working on; however, it should be pulled to the side, as shown in the 2nd image.

- Get the new yarn, then YO your hook, as shown below, then pull across your hook's last 2 loops to complete the change of color, as seen below

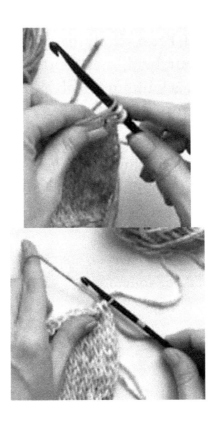

The Cowl Pattern

Note: Ensure you have gone through the notes section above and every other tips and insights discussed above before you start making this pattern.

Row 1:

- **Forward Pass:** ch 86; beginning in the 2nd chain from your hook and working in the individual chain's back bumps, grab a loop in the individual chain across=86.
- **Return Pass:**
  - YO, pulling 1 loop across on your hook
  - *YO, pulling 2 loop across on your hook
  - Repeat from* across until your hook has 1 loop

    should have an approximate measurement of 22.75" long.

Row 2:

- **Forward Pass:**

  - Work a Tks (the hook's loop)
  - Work a Tps across the individual stitch until you have 1 stitch left
  - Work a Tks into the final/ last stitch =86

- **Return Pass:**

  - YO, pulling 1 loop across on your hook
  - *YO, pulling 2 loop across on your hook

- o Repeat from* across until your hook has 1 loop

  should have an approximate measurement of 22.5" long and 0.75" tall.

Row 3:

Repeat Row 2

Row 4:

- **Forward Pass:**

  - o Work a Tks in the individual stitch across=86

- **Return Pass:**

  - o YO, pulling 1 loop across on your hook
  - o *YO, pulling 2 loop across on your hook
  - o Repeat from* across until your hook has 1 loop

Row 5-41:

Repeat Row 4

should have an approximate measurement of 12" tall.

Row 42-43:

Repeat Row 2

Bind Off

- *Slide your hook in the subsequent stitch (like the Tks)
- YO, pulling all the loops across to make a slip stitch
- Repeat from the * across
- Cut your yarn, pulling across the final/ last stitchs
- Weave the ends in before you seam

Seaming

- Using the mattress stitch, seam the cowl's back

In the end, you should have something like this below

How To Make The Mattress Stitch

Although the images at the end of this instruction is for a hat, the process is the same for a cowl. However, the instructions below are for a cowl

- Cut a piece of yarn of a length that is sufficient to seam the cowl's back.
- Use your darning needle to thread the yarn across the cowl's lower corner. Also, the yarn should be threaded across the opposite lower corner, the yarn being left loose.

- Changing to the other side, pull away the row's end stitches to show the horizontal bar that is beside the first stitch. Loosely thread the yarn across the horizontal bar.

- On the opposite side, the row's end stitches should be pulled away to show the horizontal bar that is beside the stitch, then loosely thread the yarn across.

- Grab both yarn ends, then pull the ends lightly until the seam is closed up. Weave the ends in.

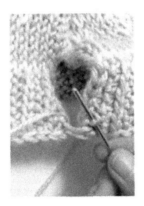

Tunisian Crochet Beanie

Materials

- 157 yd of Paintbox Yarns Wool Mix Aran. Color 811 (bright peach) was used in this project
- 6mm regular crochet hook
- 8mm Tunisian crochet hook.
- Tapestry needle
- One white pompom

Size

- This Tunisian crochet beanie is suitable for a toddler whose head measures 18-19 inches

Gauge

- 28 rows of slip stitch in 4 inches for the brim
- For the beanie's body, work the Tunisian knit stitch, 13 stitches for 14 rows in 4 inches

Notes

- The first stitch should always be skipped
- The first stitch is factored in the stitch count
- The final/ last stitch is worked below the last chain's 2 loops from the previous row.
- This pattern uses the Tunisian knit stitch

Beanie Pattern

The Brim

For this, use the Paintbox Yarns Wool Mix Aran and the 6mm regular crochet hook, ch 7, then;

1. Slip stitch into the 2nd chain from your hook and into the rest of the chains (6 stitches)
2. Ch 1, turn, then slip stitch through (6 stitches)
3. Your brim should have a height of 1.7 inches and a length of 13.75 inches

The image below displays a smaller brim compared to the one you will make; this is used to describe how the slip stitch brim should be

Body of The Beanie

For this, change to the 8mm Tunisian crochet hook

1. Ch 1; Working on the brim's long side, grab a loop from each brim's row side loops, which includes the first chain of ch 7 (94 loops on your hook), then;
   - **Work a return pass by** YO, pulling across 1 loop, then;
   - *YO, pulling across 3 loops on your hook (this closes the 2 stitches together).
   - Repeat from * for 46 times
   - YO, pulling across the final 2 loops on your hook

2. Work a Tks by sliding your hook in the 2 stitches previously closed up in the return pass. Continue in this trend for the remaining 46 stitches. The last stitch is 48 stitches. Then work a standard/ normal **return pass.**

3. Work a Tks in the individual stitch (48 stitches), then;

- Then work a standard/ normal return pass
- Continue in this manner above until your piece has a measurement of 8.5 inches in height (48 stitches)

   Note: The beanie's body will be a little bigger than the brim

4. Bind/ cast off by slip stitching into the individual stitch. For this to be neat, the individual stitch should be worked just like a Tks, but slip stitch it

rather than leaving the loops on the hook. Make allowance for a long tail for seaming the beanie.

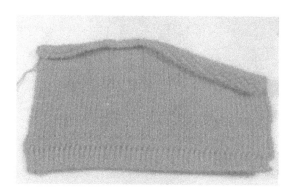

Seaming

1. Flatten your beanie with its right side facing up, then ensure the two sides that are short are folded to meet at the middle of the beanie.
2. Use the tail of the yarn you previously left and use your tapestry needle to seam (use the mattress stitch) the two short sides.
3. To avoid spaces, include the additional loop next to the side stitches (the 2nd image from the left below).

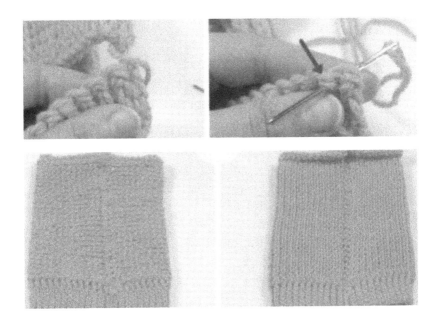

Finishing

1. Cut a yarn length, then use your tapestry needle to pull the yarn across the beanie's top chain. These chains are created when your Tunisian crochet piece is cast/bound off by slip stitching. For this to be done, change the needle's direction by going "in-out and out-in" relative to the beanie's inside.

2. After completing the round, tightly pull both ends of the yarn and seal your beanie's top. Now, affix your pompom on your beanie's top.
3. Fasten off, weaving your ends in.

Tunisian Crochet Headband

Materials

- 8mm Tunisian crochet hook
- Scissors
- Tapestry needle
- J 6mm of regular crochet hooks
- 2 colors of worsted weight yarn

Sizes

Toddler –18 - 19-inch head circumference

Child – 20 – 21-inch head circumference

Adult – 22 – 21-inch head circumference

Before You Begin

This pattern requires that you work the forward pass by yarning under rather than the usual yarning over; this makes the stitches look twisted and provides a tension that's a bit tight. However, you can yarn over as usual instead of yarning under just that due to the tension becoming looser, your headband may become a bit bigger.

The headband pattern described below is for the adult size; the sizes for a toddler and a child are in parenthesis.

Headband Pattern

1. Create a slip stitch using your Tunisian crochet hook

Row 1: Ch 15 (9, 12)

Tip: *To make a wider or lesser headband, simply adjust the no. of chains. So, if you prefer making a larger headband, use chain 17 and not chain 15.*

2. Slide your hook into the back bump of the closest stitch to your hook.

3. Pull a loop up with your yarn with 2 loops left on your hook.

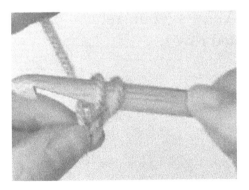

4. Keep sliding your hook into the back bumps, then pull a loop up until 16 (10, 13) loops are left on your hook. This will be your forward pass

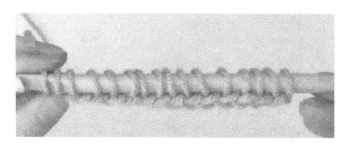

5. Pull across a loop with your yarn, which is basically your "chain up" stitch.
6. Pull across 2 loops with your yarn. Keep pulling across 2 loops with your yarn 14 (8, 11) more times. This is your return pass and you just completed row 1.

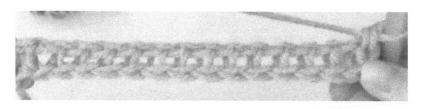

7. Row 2: Slide your hook in-between row 1's first two vertical bars and pull a loop up.

There should be 2 loops on your hook at this point.

8. Keep sliding your hook in-between the pairs of vertical bars and pulling a loop up until there are 15 (9, 12) loops left on your hook.

9. Slide your hook into Ch 1 from row 1, pulling a loop up. This will give you 16 (10, 13) loops left on your hook.

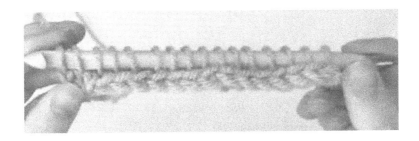

10. Pull across 1 loop with your yarn to create that Chain up we earlier talked about.

11. Pull across 2 loops with your yarn, and continue down the row for 15 times. (9, 12)

12. Repeat row 2 for rows 3-32 (26, 29)

13. Finish the forward pass for row 33 (27, 30) just as you did in previous steps. Upon making stitches for the return pass of Ch 1 and 2, cut your yarn and leave a 3-inch tail

Join your 2nd color using the special stitch method called the Magic Stitch (explained below).

Note:

- *If your 2nd color is attached during your row's return pass, the stitch will appear **inside** your headband and with this, you don't need to tie in any tails.*

- *There are 27 rows left to go (54 total) for the toddler size headband, while there are 29 rows left to go (60 total) for the child-size headband. Upon completing the no. of rows you need for the size being made, go straight to the twist instructions described below.*

- *The size of the toddler should have a measurement of roughly 14 inches long unstretched, and the size of the child should have roughly 16 inches long unstretched.*

(the Tunisian knit stitch comes with several vertical stretch)

Moving on;

14. Align your first and new yarn color ends side by side.

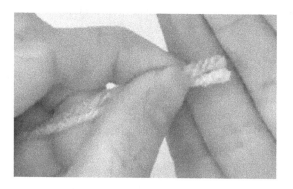

15. The new yarn color should be wrapped around your thumb twice, and below your index finger. Proceed around your yarn's two tails when making the third wrap.

16. Tuck the tail tips of your two yarn across the third wrap and below your thumb.

17. Pull your new yarn gradually to create a small knot

18. Continuously take your yarn, pulling across row 2 back down row 33.

19. Rows 34-66: Using your new yarn color, repeat row 2.

20. Cut your yarn and leave a tail of 2-foot or thereabout, tying off subsequently. The adult size should have a measurement of roughly 18 inches long unstretched.

21. Fold your headband's two ends into half, with the right side up.

22. Bring together all the ends of the four folds.

At this point, we will slip stitch all the four ends together.

23. Slide in your hook across the four ends, take up your yarn, pulling across Ch1 and all the stitches to hold in place.

24. Keep slip stitching all the four ends until you are done. Then, firmly secure or hold the ends in place by tying off. Sew your tails in and turn your headband right side out. That's all.

Chapter 5

Fixing Common Tunisian Crochet Mistakes

There is every tendency to encounter one or more mistakes when making Tunisian crochet projects, and there is no way around not coming across these mistakes. However, do not worry because I will touch on 3 of these most common mistakes you will encounter in Tunisian crochet and how you can avoid them. This section should be absolved in tandem with chapter 2 where I discussed the tips and tricks in Tunisian crochet.

Preventing a Bumpy Bottom

Nothing is more frustrating in Tunisian crochet than a bumpy bottom caused by a poorly constructed foundation row.

Extra loops float on the edge of the work due to mistakes in the foundation row, which can then snag quickly. A poor foundation row can likewise make it hard to connect motifs and making blocking to be practically impossible.

Solution

The simple remedy resides in the place you pull your foundation row loops. Begin the foundation row of the Tunisian crochet by working into the chain's back bump rather than the chain itself (as is customary in crochet). This is located when you rotate the chain to 180 degrees and then looking for the loops running along the chain's backside. Beginning with the 2nd bump from your hook, slide your hook in, pulling a loop up in the individual bump along the chain. When you work the foundation row this way, your Tunisian crochet piece will have a neat edge.

Avoiding Loopy Left Edges

The loopy left edge, like the bumpy bottom, is the result of a string of stitches that were worked improperly.

Incorrectly working the left edge results in ugly huge floating loops that could be misconstrued as a tension problem.

Solution

To achieve clean edges every time, try this simple fix: Squeeze the work within your thumb and forefinger for the final stitch of the forward pass of any Tunisian crochet stitch, as demonstrated above. Rotate the work in front of you to make the left edge visible. Pull a loop up with the hook under the two loops of the final stitch, then continue to work the return pass as directed. Working beneath the two loops of the final stitch ensures uniformity and eliminates tension concerns.

Fixing Curling

In chapter 2, we briefly touched on the tips and tricks to fix curling issues. Let's go a little deeper in this section

Curling is virtually everyone's main problem when learning Tunisian crochet.

While working on your projects, the fabric of your Tunisian crochet will likely curl inwardly at the top and bottom edges, and there isn't much you can do about it. As you complete more rows, the curling will occur when you repeatedly draw the stitches forward.

Solution

Choosing the appropriate hook size is the first attempt against curling. Choosing a hook 1-2mm bigger than the ball band your yarn advises is a good rule of thumb to learn early on.

For instance, if a DK weight, category 3 yarn asks for a 4mm crochet hook, start with a 5.5mm crochet hook to evaluate how the gauge and tension will feel for the piece you're planning. The tension on each stitch loosens when the hook size is increased, allowing the yarn to relax a little.

If everything else fails, blocking a completed Tunisian crochet piece is the most effective technique to get rid of the curl. Blocking adds moisture to the mix while also assisting fibers (particularly animal fibers) in their behavior.

Spray blocking is the simplest way of blocking. Lay your work on a clean foam play mat or, preferably, a blocking board to start off. Rust-proof pins are then used to hold the piece down. Warm water should be sprayed uniformly across the piece. Allow the piece to dry completely after it has been dampened. To expedite the process, place the blocking board beneath a ceiling fan.

Pro tip: Use Soak Flatter Spray to provide fragrance to your blocking procedure. The gently fragrant Soak Flatter Spray leaves Tunisian crochet projects silky and static-free.

The End... Almost!

Hey! We've made it to the final chapter of this book, and I hope you've enjoyed it so far.

If you have not done so yet, I would be incredibly thankful if you could take just a minute to leave a quick review on Amazon

Reviews are not easy to come by, and as an independent author with a little marketing budget, I rely on you, my readers, to leave a short review on Amazon.

Even if it is just a sentence or two!

So if you really enjoyed this book, please...

>> Click here to leave a brief review on Amazon.

I truly appreciate your effort to leave your review, as it truly makes a huge difference.

Chapter 6

Tunisian Crochet FAQs

This chapter covers a cross-section of the frequently asked questions beginners usually ask. So, let's get right into a couple of such basic questions.

Can A Conventional Crochet Hook Be Used For Tunisian Crochet?

You can use the regular or traditional crochet hook for Tunisian crochet, but this will be restricted to smaller projects and unsuitable for bigger projects. The reason is that it becomes harder to fit all the stitches of bigger projects on a regular crochet hook. Tunisian crochet hooks have two characteristics that make holding more stitches simpler. The first is that the hooks of Tunisian crochet are longer than the hooks of regular crochet, and the second is that the ends of their hooks come with stoppers.

Is Tunisian Crochet Easy?

The answer is YES. Tunisian crochet is not just easy, but very easy. Although it is more helpful if there is an onsite tutor to make the learning process seamless. Nevertheless, you can also learn Tunisian crochet all by yourself with the help of a practical guide like the one you are using currently. Practicing and gaining mastery of some fundamental The techniques of Tunisian crochet makes it more easy to learn and implement the stitches.

Before moving to more advanced stitching techniques, try to practice and master the easier stitches, making it easy to learn other stitching techniques. This is because mastering the simple stitches will get you accustomed to the basic hand motions.

Which Is Faster: Tunisian Crochet Or Knitting?

Tunisian crochet is practically faster than knitting, but that's only if you're well experienced in the technique. As you gain more experience with time in the craft, you will discover that Tunisian crochet tends to be faster than regular crochet and closely twice as fast as knitting.

How Can Curling Be Stopped In Tunisian Crochet?

I guess we have over flogged this aspect, but it keeps coming up because it's one of the major problems faced in Tunisian crochet. So, in addition to all the tips and hints discussed about fixing curling issues, there are a couple more things you can do if none of what has been discussed works.

Troubleshooter #1: Make seams: Good news! Running seams across the borders of a completed Tunisian Crochet work eradicates the curling. If the seams are for Crochet pieces like scarves, you need not worry because they would make it curl-free instantly.

Troubleshooter #2: Ensure that you reduce the tension that lines up the edges of your project. Loosening up your work will help reduce the curls along the borders of your project. Your work will still be curled but not as terrible as it would be with a tight tension.

In all the curling fixing methods discussed so far, blocking is the most preferable.

What Can Tunisian Crochet Be Used To Make?

The style involved in Tunisian crochet can mostly cover anything and everything. However, it all depends on your creativity. Here are a handful of projects that Tunisian crochet styles are great for.

- Headbands

- Afghans

- Shawls

- Baby blankets

- Beanies

- Blankets

- Sweaters

- Pillows

- Bags

- Scarves

Why Is My Tunisian Crochet Slanting?

You must realize that your work can slant on one side, especially the left. As a beginner, you must understand that slanting is totally normal and doesn't mean you might have gotten something wrong. So, you need not feel discouraged. Nonetheless, we'd list a couple of things you can do to mitigate against it.

- Keep a consistent tension
- Firmly secure the first stitch (or chain)

- Free up the last stitch

After doing any of the above and you still have slanting issues, then;

- Block your work.

Conclusion

From the chapters discussed so far, you must have realized that Tunisian-styled Crochet pieces are easy to make. Fabrics produced from them are thick, spongy, and very beautiful. They are a perfect choice for cowls, dishcloths, potholders, beanies, ear warmers, and lots more. You've learned how to manipulate yarns, colors, and stitches to produce beautiful Tunisian crochet designs. The concepts of charts, symbols, abbreviations, Tunisian crochet tips and tricks, and several insightful techniques were also discussed to help you evolve from a beginner into a pro. And in the journey so far traveled, I hope that you have realized no adventure is void of challenges, hence the need for chapter 6, which touched on a couple of challenges you might experience with guidance on how to mitigate against them.

For this book to be useful to you, it is expedient you practice again and again. Nobody becomes a master by observation, but by consistent practice. Also, always take out time to make researches to improve your skills and in a short while, you will be amazed at the pieces your hands can produce with Tunisian crochet.

I wish you all the best!

CPSIA information can be obtained
at www.ICGtesting.com
Printed in the USA
BVHW050537140223
658474BV00002B/69

9 781955 935340